THE URBANA FREE LIBRARY
3 1230 00984 8900

W9-AXG-739
DISCARDED BY THE
URBANA FREE LIBRARY
The Urbana Free Library
To renew: call 217-367-4057
or go to urbanafreelibrary.org
and select My Account

*In 1776, the founders of the United States of America declared that consent of the governed would be a key component of our country. The founders didn't always agree on everything, but they did all believe that the power of our government should come from the will of the people and that citizens would express their choices by voting in elections.*

*But at that time, only some people were allowed to vote. Citizenship (the legal status of being a member of a country) and the right to vote (sometimes called the franchise, political franchise, or suffrage) were not available to all.*

*As our nation grew, our understanding of democracy and rights grew too. Many people stood up and spoke up about abolition (the end of slavery), about citizenship, about enfranchisement, and about civil rights (equal opportunity for all). They also worked to end voter suppression (the practice of discouraging or preventing people from voting).*

*They heard equality's call. . . .*

# EQUALITY'S CALL

## THE STORY OF VOTING RIGHTS IN AMERICA

written by Deborah Diesen illustrated by Magdalena Mora

Beach Lane Books • New York London Toronto Sydney New Delhi

VOTING
RIGHTS

Our founders declared
When our country began
That consent of the governed
Was part of the plan.

Through voting, elections,
And representation,
The voice of the people
Would strengthen our nation.

In fact, though, for years
This great founding ideal
Was extended to some
And for others not real.

*But we heard in the distance*
*Equality's call:*

*A right isn't right*
*Till it's granted to all.*

The states set the rules
About who got to vote;
And your gender, your race,
And your wealth were of note.

COULD VOTE

COULD NOT VOTE

White men with property
Went to the polls,
But the rest of the people
Were left off the rolls.

The dream of democracy
Wasn't yet true.
There were changes to make.
There was work still to do.

*But we heard growing clearer*
*Equality's call:*

*A right isn't right*
*Till it's granted to all.*

AMERICAN
HISTORY

The rules about wealth
Were the first thing to go.
As more were enfranchised,
Their voices could grow.

And a small group of voices
Was raising the fact
That enslavement was wrong—
An unspeakable act.

VOTES FOR WOMEN
THE VOTING RIGHTS ACT
1965
SOJOURNER TRUTH: A BIOGRAPHY
SOJOURNER TRUTH: A BIOGRAPHY

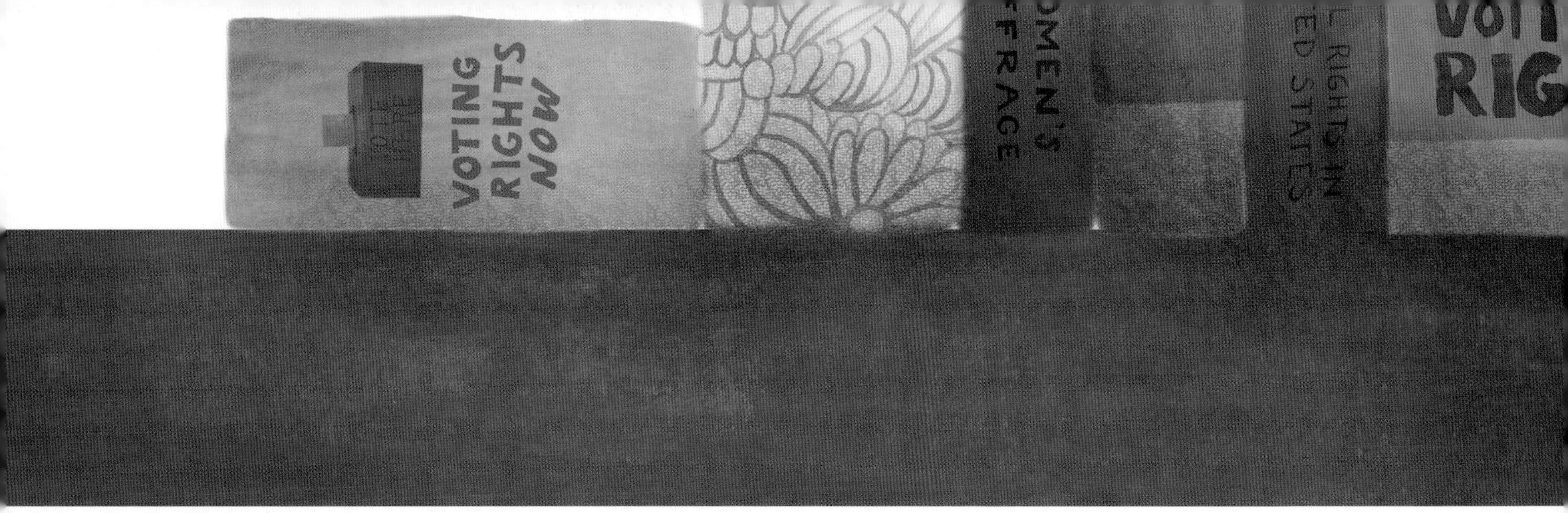


Good people stood up
For the truth that they knew:
Abolition and suffrage
Were long overdue.

*We heard ever louder*
*Equality's call:*

*A right isn't right*
*Till it's granted to all.*

There was war in our nation
And slavery ended.
Amendments were added,
The franchise extended.

VOTE
HERE

Now more men could vote—
At least so the law said,
Yet denial through taxes
And tests was widespread.

And the voices of women
Were mostly omitted.
In only some states
Was their voting permitted.

*But nothing could muffle*
*Equality's call:*

Give us the

*A right isn't right*
*Till it's granted to all.*

Suffragists didn't
Give up on the fight,
And the Nineteenth Amendment
Gave women the right.

But voters of color
Still met with oppression.
Their voting was hindered
By brutal suppression.

So we passed legislation
To make voting fair,

1965

SELMA TO MONTGOMERY MARCH / VOTING RIGHTS ACT IS PASSED

To extend and protect
Voters' rights everywhere.

1970

FIRST EXTENSION OF VOTING RIGHTS ACT

NOW
WE DEMAND
EQUALITY
NOW!
WHAT
WILL YOU DO
FOR
WOMAN
SUFFRAGE?

*We heard it, we felt it,*
*Equality's call:*

*A right isn't right*
*Till it's granted to all.*

The journey's not over.
The work hasn't ended.
Democracy's dream
Must be constantly tended.

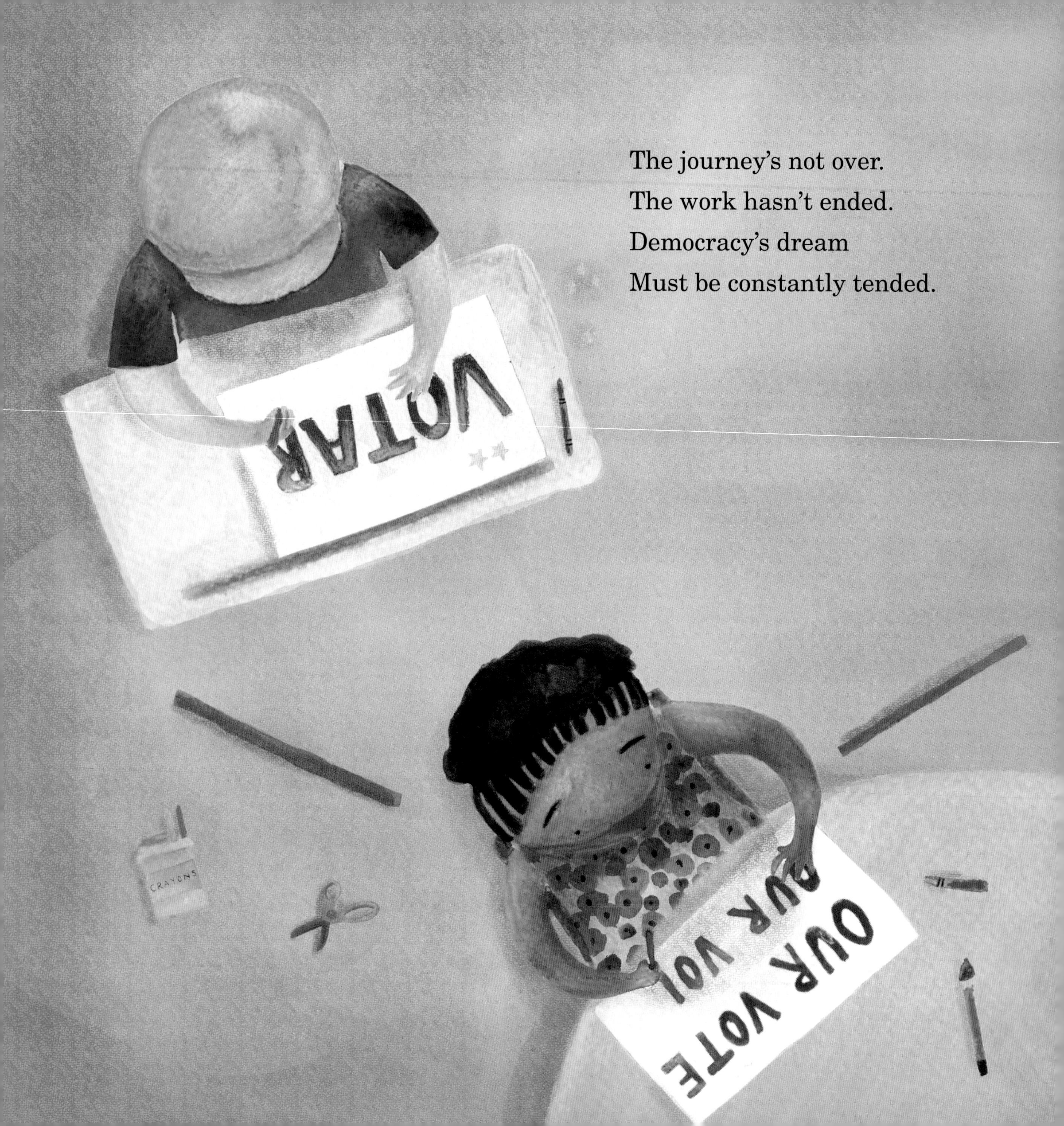

But where we are now
Is a debt that we owe
To the work of more people
Than ever we'll know.

And each time we vote,
We acknowledge that past.
We honor our rights
To ensure they will last.

*For to vote is to answer*
*Equality's call.*
*And each time we vote . . .*

*We vote with them all.*

VOTE
WE DEMAND
EQUALITY NOW!
OUR VOTE OUR VOICE
VOTING IS PEOPLE POWER
TU VOTO ES TU VOZ
WE DEMAND
VOTING RIGHTS NOW!

# VOTING-RELATED AMENDMENTS & LEGISLATION

The U.S. Constitution, ratified in 1788, is our nation's framework and fundamental law. As originally written, it did not establish voting rights. It allowed states to determine who was eligible to vote. Since then, constitutional amendments and federal laws have been passed to extend citizenship and voting rights and to protect those rights from being violated. Some key amendments and laws include:

**Fifteenth Amendment** *(ratified 1870)—granted African American men the right to vote*
After the Civil War, the Thirteenth Amendment abolished slavery, the Fourteenth Amendment granted citizenship to former slaves, and the Fifteenth Amendment affirmed the right of African American men to vote. However, after passage of the Fifteenth Amendment, some states enacted laws that created discriminatory barriers to voting, such as literacy tests and poll taxes. Jim Crow laws and intimidation tactics, including violence, suppressed black voting, especially in Southern states.

**Nineteenth Amendment** *(ratified 1920)—granted women the right to vote*
At the time the Nineteenth Amendment was ratified, many Americans, including Native Americans and Asian Americans, were prevented from becoming citizens. Only women who were citizens gained the right to vote when the Nineteenth Amendment went into effect, and only those with access to the polls were able to cast votes.

**The Indian Citizenship Act** *(1924)—granted citizenship to Native Americans*
Though this act granted Native Americans U.S. citizenship, laws in some states continued to prevent Native Americans from voting. Native Americans did not gain voting rights in all states until 1957.

**The Chinese Exclusion Repeal Act** *(1943)—granted citizenship to some Chinese immigrants; and* **The Immigration and Nationality Act** *(1952)—ended Asian-American citizenship restrictions*
Prior to these acts, most Asian Americans had been prevented from becoming U.S. citizens by the Naturalization Act of 1790 and the Chinese Exclusion Act of 1882. Unable to become citizens, they were also unable to vote.

**Twenty-Third Amendment** *(ratified 1961)—gave residents of Washington DC the right to vote for president and vice president*
The representation of citizens living in the District of Columbia is different than that of citizens living in the fifty states. The District elects a nonvoting delegate to the U.S. House of Representatives but has no representation in the U.S. Senate. Prior to the Twenty-Third Amendment, DC residents were not able to vote in presidential elections.

**Twenty-Fourth Amendment** *(ratified 1964)—outlawed the poll tax in federal elections*
Poll taxes were a fee that had to be paid prior to

voting, and they restricted voting for the poor. Poll taxes were levied in some states from the 1890s until the 1960s, and their primary intent was to disenfranchise black voters. The Twenty-Fourth Amendment abolished the poll tax in federal elections. Some states continued to impose poll taxes for state elections, until the Supreme Court declared them unconstitutional in 1966.

**The Voting Rights Act** *(1965)—outlawed discriminatory voting rules such as literacy tests*
An act to enforce the Fifteenth Amendment, the Voting Rights Act prohibited racially discriminatory state and local barriers to voter registration and voting. It also provided for more oversight of state and local voting practices. Although intended to be a temporary or emergency measure, renewals and changes to the Voting Rights Act (in 1970, 1975, 1982, 1992, and 2006) extended and improved voting protections, including a requirement for bilingual voting materials in some communities. A Supreme Court decision in 2013 (*Shelby County v. Holder*) struck down a key provision of the Voting Rights Act. Since then many states have enacted new barriers to voting, such as voter ID requirements and restrictions on voter registration.

**Twenty-Sixth Amendment** *(ratified 1971)—lowered the voting age from 21 to 18*
In the 1970 extension to the Voting Rights Act, Congress had lowered the voting age to 18, but in that same year, the Supreme Court had ruled that the law was only valid for federal elections. The Twenty-Sixth Amendment guaranteed the right to vote at age 18 in all elections.

**Voting Accessibility for the Elderly and Handicapped Act** *(1984)—improved physical access to voting*
This act required states to assure that polling places were accessible. Accessibility requirements were furthered by Title II of the 1990 Americans with Disabilities Act, which ensured that people with disabilities have the full and equal opportunity to vote.

**The National Voter Registration Act** *(1993)—required states to expand voter registration opportunities*
Also known as the Motor Voter Act, this act made it easier for Americans to register to vote, including when obtaining or renewing a driver's license.

**Help America Vote Act** *(2002)—made reforms to the election system*
This act established state voting standards and provided funding to states to improve their voting equipment.

This list is not exhaustive. Voting rights have been impacted by other federal laws, by Supreme Court decisions, and by state laws. The effort to protect voting rights is ongoing. To learn more, head on over to your library. You can also visit deborahdiesen.com for further reading suggestions.

# VOTING RIGHTS ACTIVISTS

Throughout our nation's history, many people have spoken up for the right to vote. Speaking up was not easy. Sometimes it was even dangerous. But the call of equality could not be ignored. People answered the call by standing up for what they believed in. Their voices, their actions, and their commitment to the cause led to important changes. The following are some of the many people who have influenced voting rights in this country. The people listed in bold appear in the pages of this book.

Jane Addams (1860–1935)—Social reformer, suffragist

**Susan B. Anthony** (1820–1906)—Abolitionist, suffragist

Joaquin Avila (1948–2018)—Civil rights activist

Ella Baker (1903–1986)—Civil rights activist

Henry Ward Beecher (1813–1887)—Abolitionist

Mary McLeod Bethune (1875–1955)—Civil rights activist

Olympia Brown (1835–1926)—Suffragist

Lucy Burns (1879–1966)—Suffragist

Evelyn Thomas Butts (1924–1993)—Civil rights activist, politician

Mary Ann Shadd Cary (1823–1893)—Abolitionist, suffragist

**Carrie Chapman Catt** (1859–1947)—Suffragist

Cesar Chavez (1927–1993)—Civil rights activist

Septima Poinsette Clark (1898–1987)—Civil rights activist

**Anna Julia Cooper** (1858–1964)—Civil rights activist, suffragist

Frederick Douglass (c. 1818–1895)—Abolitionist, suffragist, social reformer, statesman

Wilhelmina Kekelaokalaninui Widemann Dowsett (1861–1929)—Suffragist

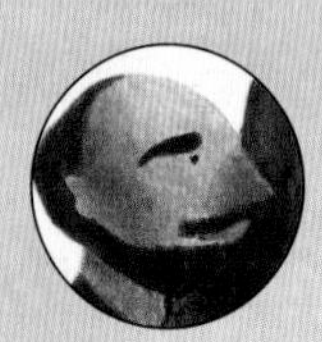

**W. E. B. Du Bois** (1868–1963)—Civil rights activist

Rosanell Eaton (1921–2018)—Civil rights activist

Benjamin Franklin (1706–1790)—Founder, statesman

Matilda Joslyn Gage (1826–1898)—Abolitionist, suffragist

William Lloyd Garrison (1805–1879)—Abolitionist, suffragist

Charlotte Forten Grimké (1837–1914)—Abolitionist, suffragist

**Fannie Lou Hamer** (1917–1977)—Civil rights activist

Frances E. W. Harper (1825–1911)—Abolitionist, suffragist

Julia Ward Howe (1819–1910)—Abolitionist, suffragist

**Dolores Huerta** (born 1930)—Civil rights activist

**Thomas Jefferson** (1743–1826)—Founder, third president

**Martin Luther King Jr.** (1929–1968)—Civil rights activist

Fred Korematsu (1919–2005)—Civil rights activist

**Mabel Ping-Hua Lee** (1896–1966)—Suffragist

**John Lewis** (b. 1940)—Civil rights activist, politician

**Abraham Lincoln** (1809–1865)—Sixteenth president

**James Madison** (1751–1836)—Founder, fourth president

Inez Milholland (1886–1916)—Suffragist

Lucretia Mott (1793–1880)—Abolitionist, suffragist

Adelina Otero-Warren (1881–1965)—Suffragist, politician

**Alice Paul** (1885–1977)—Suffragist

Harriet Forten Purvis (1810–1875)—Abolitionist, suffragist

Sarah Parker Remond (1826–1894)—Abolitionist, suffragist

Ed Roberts (1939–1995)—Disability rights activist

Amelia Boynton Robinson (1911–2015)—Civil rights activist

**Josephine St. Pierre Ruffin** (1842–1924)—Suffragist, civil rights activist

Abby Hadassah Smith (1797–1878)—Suffragist

Julia Evelina Smith (1792–1886)—Suffragist

Elizabeth Cady Stanton (1815–1902)—Abolitionist, suffragist

Thaddeus Stevens (1792–1868)—Abolitionist, politician

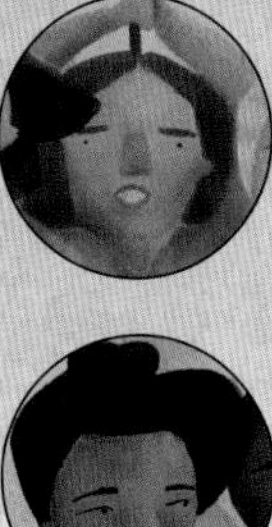

**Lucy Stone** (1818–1893)—Abolitionist, suffragist

Charles Sumner (1811–1874)—Abolitionist, politician

**Mary Church Terrell** (1863–1954)—Civil rights activist, suffragist

Susette LaFlesche Tibbles (1854–1903)—Civil rights activist

William Trotter (1872–1934)—Civil rights activist

Miguel Trujillo (1904–1989)—Civil rights activist

**Sojourner Truth** (c. 1797–1883)—Abolitionist, suffragist

Harriet Tubman (c. 1820–1913)—Abolitionist, suffragist

Willie Velasquez (1944–1988)—Civil rights activist

**George Washington** (1732–1799)—Founder, first president

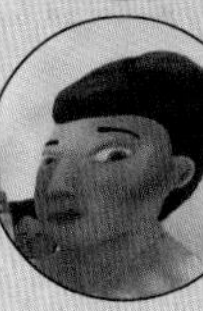

**Ida B. Wells-Barnett** (1862–1931)—Civil rights activist, suffragist

Wong Chin Foo (1847–1898)—Civil rights activist

Zitkala-Ša (1876–1938)—Civil rights activist

How will *you* answer equality's call?

*For Mason and Isaac—D. D.*

*To Lorraine and both Juans—M. M.*

*The author is grateful for the invaluable input and assistance of historian Marsha Barrett. Any mistakes are my own.*

*The illustrator is grateful for the input of historians Juan Mora-Torres, Juan I. Mora, and Carolina Ortega.*

BEACH LANE BOOKS • An imprint of Simon & Schuster Children's Publishing Division • 1230 Avenue of the Americas, New York, New York 10020 • Text copyright

For information about special discounts for bulk purchases, please contact Simon & Schuster Special Sales at 1-866-506-1949 or business@simonandschuster.com. • The Simon & Schuster Speakers Bureau can bring authors to your live event. For more information or to book an event, contact the Simon & Schuster Speakers Bureau at 1-866-248-3049 or visit our website at www.simonspeakers.com. • Book design by Lauren Rille • The text for this book was set in New Century Schoolbook. • The illustrations for this book were rendered in gouache, watercolor, ink, pastel, pencil, and digital collage. • Manufactured in China • 1119 SCP • First Edition • 10 9 8 7 6 5 4 3 2 1 • Library of Congress Cataloging-in-Publication Data • Names: Diesen, Deborah, author. | Mora, Magdalena, 1991– illustrator. • Title: Equality's call / Deborah Diesen ; illustrated by Magdalena Mora. • Description: First edition. | New York : Beach Lane Books, [2020] | Includes bibliographical references and index. | Audience: Ages: 3 to 8. | Audience: Grades: K to grade 3. | Summary: "A powerful look at the evolution of voting rights in the United States, from our nation's founding to the present day"—Provided by publisher. • Identifiers: LCCN 2019009579 | ISBN 9781534439580 (hardcover : alk. paper) | ISBN 9781534439597 (eBook) • Subjects: LCSH: Suffrage—United States—History—Juvenile literature. • Classification: LCC JK1846.D54 2020 | DDC 324.6/20973—dc23 • LC record available at https://lccn.loc.gov/2019009579